Complete Inspirational

Executive
Daily Planner
and
Appointment
Book

Activinotes

Activinotes

DAILY JOURNALS, PLANNERS, NOTEBOOKS AND OTHER BLANK BOOKS

Executive Daily Planner and
Appointment Book

date
_____

time	task	status

to do list:

_____ ☐
_____ ☐
_____ ☐
_____ ☐
_____ ☐
_____ ☐
_____ ☐
_____ ☐
                        ☐

notes:

Executive Daily Planner and
Appointment Book

date
_____

time	task	status

to do list:

_____ ☐
_____ ☐
_____ ☐
_____ ☐
_____ ☐
_____ ☐
_____ ☐
_____ ☐
_____ ☐

notes:

Executive Daily Planner and Appointment Book

date
_____

time	task	status

to do list:

_____ ☐
_____ ☐
_____ ☐
_____ ☐
_____ ☐
_____ ☐
_____ ☐
_____ ☐
_____ ☐

notes:

Executive Daily Planner and
Appointment Book

time	task	status

to do list:

_____ ☐
_____ ☐
_____ ☐
_____ ☐
_____ ☐
_____ ☐
_____ ☐
_____ ☐
_____ ☐

notes:

Executive Daily Planner and
Appointment Book

time	task	status

to do list:

_____

_____

_____

_____

_____

_____

_____

_____

notes:

Executive Daily Planner and
Appointment Book

date

time	task	status

to do list:

☐
☐
☐
☐
☐
☐
☐
☐
☐

notes:

Executive Daily Planner and
Appointment Book

date
_____

time	task	status

to do list:

_____ ☐
_____ ☐
_____ ☐
_____ ☐
_____ ☐
_____ ☐
_____ ☐
_____ ☐
_____ ☐

notes:

Executive Daily Planner and Appointment Book

date
_____

time	task	status

to do list:

_____ ☐
_____ ☐
_____ ☐
_____ ☐
_____ ☐
_____ ☐
_____ ☐
_____ ☐
_____ ☐

notes:

Executive Daily Planner and
Appointment Book

time	task	status

to do list:

_____ ☐
_____ ☐
_____ ☐
_____ ☐
_____ ☐
_____ ☐
_____ ☐
_____ ☐
_____ ☐

notes:

Executive Daily Planner and
Appointment Book

date
___

time	task	status

to do list:

_____ ☐
_____ ☐
_____ ☐
_____ ☐
_____ ☐
_____ ☐
_____ ☐
_____ ☐
_____ ☐

notes:

Executive Daily Planner and
Appointment Book

date ____

time	task	status

to do list:

_____ ☐
_____ ☐
_____ ☐
_____ ☐
_____ ☐
_____ ☐
_____ ☐
_____ ☐
_____ ☐

notes:

Executive Daily Planner and
Appointment Book

time	task	status

to do list:

_____ ☐
_____ ☐
_____ ☐
_____ ☐
_____ ☐
_____ ☐
_____ ☐
_____ ☐
_____ ☐

notes:

Executive Daily Planner and
Appointment Book

time	task	status

to do list:

- ☐
- ☐
- ☐
- ☐
- ☐
- ☐
- ☐
- ☐
- ☐

notes:

Executive Daily Planner and
Appointment Book

date
_____

time	task	status

to do list:

_____ ☐
_____ ☐
_____ ☐
_____ ☐
_____ ☐
_____ ☐
_____ ☐
_____ ☐
_____ ☐

notes:

Executive Daily Planner and
Appointment Book

date
____

time	task	status

to do list:

_____ ☐
_____ ☐
_____ ☐
_____ ☐
_____ ☐
_____ ☐
_____ ☐
_____ ☐
_____ ☐

notes:

Executive Daily Planner and
Appointment Book

date
_____

time	task	status

to do list:

_____ ☐
_____ ☐
_____ ☐
_____ ☐
_____ ☐
_____ ☐
_____ ☐
_____ ☐
_____ ☐

notes:

Executive Daily Planner and
Appointment Book

date
____

time	task	status

to do list:

_____ ☐
_____ ☐
_____ ☐
_____ ☐
_____ ☐
_____ ☐
_____ ☐
_____ ☐
_____ ☐

notes:

Executive Daily Planner and
Appointment Book

date

time	task	status

to do list:

☐
☐
☐
☐
☐
☐
☐
☐
☐

notes:

Executive Daily Planner and
Appointment Book

date

time	task	status

to do list:

☐
☐
☐
☐
☐
☐
☐
☐
☐

notes:

Executive Daily Planner and
Appointment Book

date
_____

time	task	status

to do list:

_____ ☐
_____ ☐
_____ ☐
_____ ☐
_____ ☐
_____ ☐
_____ ☐
_____ ☐

notes:

Executive Daily Planner and
Appointment Book

date
_____

time	task	status

to do list:

_____ ☐
_____ ☐
_____ ☐
_____ ☐
_____ ☐
_____ ☐
_____ ☐
_____ ☐
_____ ☐

notes:

Executive Daily Planner and
Appointment Book

time	task	status

to do list:

_____ ☐
_____ ☐
_____ ☐
_____ ☐
_____ ☐
_____ ☐
_____ ☐
_____ ☐
_____ ☐

notes:

Executive Daily Planner and
Appointment Book

date
_____

time	task	status

to do list:

_____ ☐
_____ ☐
_____ ☐
_____ ☐
_____ ☐
_____ ☐
_____ ☐
_____ ☐
_____ ☐

notes:

Executive Daily Planner and
Appointment Book

date

time	task	status

to do list:

_____ ☐
_____ ☐
_____ ☐
_____ ☐
_____ ☐
_____ ☐
_____ ☐
_____ ☐
_____ ☐

notes:

Executive Daily Planner and
Appointment Book

date _____

time	task	status

to do list:

_____ ☐
_____ ☐
_____ ☐
_____ ☐
_____ ☐
_____ ☐
_____ ☐
_____ ☐
_____ ☐

notes:

Executive Daily Planner and
Appointment Book

date

time	task	status

to do list:

_____ ☐
_____ ☐
_____ ☐
_____ ☐
_____ ☐
_____ ☐
_____ ☐
_____ ☐
_____ ☐

notes:

Executive Daily Planner and
Appointment Book

date

time	task	status

to do list:

_____ ☐
_____ ☐
_____ ☐
_____ ☐
_____ ☐
_____ ☐
_____ ☐
_____ ☐
_____ ☐

notes:

Executive Daily Planner and
Appointment Book

date
_____

time	task	status

to do list:

_____ ☐
_____ ☐
_____ ☐
_____ ☐
_____ ☐
_____ ☐
_____ ☐
_____ ☐
_____ ☐

notes:

Executive Daily Planner and Appointment Book

date
_____

time	task	status

to do list:

_____ ☐
_____ ☐
_____ ☐
_____ ☐
_____ ☐
_____ ☐
_____ ☐
_____ ☐
_____ ☐

notes:

Executive Daily Planner and
Appointment Book

time	task	status

to do list:

☐
☐
☐
☐
☐
☐
☐
☐
☐

notes:

Executive Daily Planner and
Appointment Book

date

time	task	status

to do list:

_____ ☐
_____ ☐
_____ ☐
_____ ☐
_____ ☐
_____ ☐
_____ ☐
_____ ☐
_____ ☐

notes:

Executive Daily Planner and Appointment Book

date
_____

time	task	status

to do list:

_____ ☐
_____ ☐
_____ ☐
_____ ☐
_____ ☐
_____ ☐
_____ ☐
_____ ☐
_____ ☐

notes:

Executive Daily Planner and
Appointment Book

_____ date

time	task	status

to do list:

_____ ☐
_____ ☐
_____ ☐
_____ ☐
_____ ☐
_____ ☐
_____ ☐
_____ ☐
_____ ☐

notes:

Executive Daily Planner and Appointment Book

date

time	task	status

to do list:

_____ ☐
_____ ☐
_____ ☐
_____ ☐
_____ ☐
_____ ☐
_____ ☐
_____ ☐
_____ ☐

notes:

Executive Daily Planner and
Appointment Book

date
____

time	task	status

to do list:

_____ ☐
_____ ☐
_____ ☐
_____ ☐
_____ ☐
_____ ☐
_____ ☐
_____ ☐
_____ ☐

notes:

Executive Daily Planner and
Appointment Book

time	task	status

to do list:

_____ ☐
_____ ☐
_____ ☐
_____ ☐
_____ ☐
_____ ☐
_____ ☐
_____ ☐
_____ ☐

notes:

Executive Daily Planner and
Appointment Book

date
_____

time	task	status

to do list:

_____ ☐
_____ ☐
_____ ☐
_____ ☐
_____ ☐
_____ ☐
_____ ☐
_____ ☐
_____ ☐

notes:

Executive Daily Planner and
Appointment Book

time	task	status

to do list:

_____ ☐
_____ ☐
_____ ☐
_____ ☐
_____ ☐
_____ ☐
_____ ☐
_____ ☐
_____ ☐

notes:

Executive Daily Planner and
Appointment Book

date

time	task	status

to do list:

_____ ☐
_____ ☐
_____ ☐
_____ ☐
_____ ☐
_____ ☐
_____ ☐
_____ ☐
_____ ☐

notes:

Executive Daily Planner and
Appointment Book

time	task	status

to do list:

☐
☐
☐
☐
☐
☐
☐
☐
☐

notes:

Executive Daily Planner and
Appointment Book

date
_____

time	task	status

to do list:

_____ ☐
_____ ☐
_____ ☐
_____ ☐
_____ ☐
_____ ☐
_____ ☐
_____ ☐
_____ ☐

notes:

Executive Daily Planner and
Appointment Book

date
_____

time	task	status

to do list:

_____ ☐
_____ ☐
_____ ☐
_____ ☐
_____ ☐
_____ ☐
_____ ☐
_____ ☐
_____ ☐

notes:

Executive Daily Planner and
Appointment Book

date ___

time	task	status

to do list:

_____ ☐
_____ ☐
_____ ☐
_____ ☐
_____ ☐
_____ ☐
_____ ☐
_____ ☐
_____ ☐

notes:

Executive Daily Planner and Appointment Book

date

time	task	status

to do list:

_____ ☐
_____ ☐
_____ ☐
_____ ☐
_____ ☐
_____ ☐
_____ ☐
_____ ☐
_____ ☐

notes:

Executive Daily Planner and
Appointment Book

date _____

time	task	status

to do list:

_____ ☐
_____ ☐
_____ ☐
_____ ☐
_____ ☐
_____ ☐
_____ ☐
_____ ☐
_____ ☐

notes:

Executive Daily Planner and
Appointment Book

time	task	status

to do list:

_____ ☐
_____ ☐
_____ ☐
_____ ☐
_____ ☐
_____ ☐
_____ ☐
_____ ☐
_____ ☐

notes:

Executive Daily Planner and
Appointment Book

time	task	status

to do list:

___ ☐
___ ☐
___ ☐
___ ☐
___ ☐
___ ☐
___ ☐
___ ☐

notes:

Executive Daily Planner and
Appointment Book

date

time	task	status

to do list:

- [ ] _____
- [ ] _____
- [ ] _____
- [ ] _____
- [ ] _____
- [ ] _____
- [ ] _____
- [ ] _____
- [ ] _____

notes:

Executive Daily Planner and
Appointment Book

date
_____

time	task	status

to do list:

_____ ☐
_____ ☐
_____ ☐
_____ ☐
_____ ☐
_____ ☐
_____ ☐
_____ ☐
_____ ☐

notes:

Executive Daily Planner and
Appointment Book

date

time	task	status

to do list:

☐
☐
☐
☐
☐
☐
☐
☐
☐

notes:

Executive Daily Planner and
Appointment Book

date ____

time	task	status

to do list:

_____ ☐
_____ ☐
_____ ☐
_____ ☐
_____ ☐
_____ ☐
_____ ☐
_____ ☐
_____ ☐

notes:

Executive Daily Planner and
Appointment Book

date
_____

time	task	status

to do list:

_____ ☐
_____ ☐
_____ ☐
_____ ☐
_____ ☐
_____ ☐
_____ ☐
_____ ☐
_____ ☐

notes:

Executive Daily Planner and
Appointment Book

date
_____

time	task	status

to do list:

_____ ☐
_____ ☐
_____ ☐
_____ ☐
_____ ☐
_____ ☐
_____ ☐
_____ ☐
_____ ☐

notes:

Executive Daily Planner and
Appointment Book

date

time	task	status

to do list:

☐
☐
☐
☐
☐
☐
☐
☐
☐

notes:

Executive Daily Planner and
Appointment Book

date
_____

time	task	status

to do list:

_____ ☐
_____ ☐
_____ ☐
_____ ☐
_____ ☐
_____ ☐
_____ ☐
_____ ☐
_____ ☐

notes:

Executive Daily Planner and
Appointment Book

date

time	task	status

to do list:

_____ ☐
_____ ☐
_____ ☐
_____ ☐
_____ ☐
_____ ☐
_____ ☐
_____ ☐
_____ ☐

notes:

Executive Daily Planner and
Appointment Book

date
____

time	task	status

to do list:

_____ ☐
_____ ☐
_____ ☐
_____ ☐
_____ ☐
_____ ☐
_____ ☐
_____ ☐
_____ ☐

notes:

Executive Daily Planner and
Appointment Book

date
_____

time	task	status

to do list:

_____ ☐
_____ ☐
_____ ☐
_____ ☐
_____ ☐
_____ ☐
_____ ☐
_____ ☐
_____ ☐

notes:

Executive Daily Planner and
Appointment Book

date
_____

time	task	status

to do list:

_____ ☐
_____ ☐
_____ ☐
_____ ☐
_____ ☐
_____ ☐
_____ ☐
_____ ☐
_____ ☐

notes:

Executive Daily Planner and
Appointment Book

date
_____

time	task	status

to do list:

_____ ☐
_____ ☐
_____ ☐
_____ ☐
_____ ☐
_____ ☐
_____ ☐
_____ ☐
_____ ☐

notes:

Executive Daily Planner and
Appointment Book

date _____

time	task	status

to do list:

_____ ☐
_____ ☐
_____ ☐
_____ ☐
_____ ☐
_____ ☐
_____ ☐
_____ ☐
_____ ☐

notes:

Executive Daily Planner and
Appointment Book

date
_____

time	task	status

to do list:

_____ ☐
_____ ☐
_____ ☐
_____ ☐
_____ ☐
_____ ☐
_____ ☐
_____ ☐
_____ ☐

notes:

Executive Daily Planner and
Appointment Book

time	task	status

to do list:

___ ☐
___ ☐
___ ☐
___ ☐
___ ☐
___ ☐
___ ☐
___ ☐
  ☐

notes:

Executive Daily Planner and
Appointment Book

date

time	task	status

to do list:

_____ ☐
_____ ☐
_____ ☐
_____ ☐
_____ ☐
_____ ☐
_____ ☐
_____ ☐
_____ ☐

notes:

Executive Daily Planner and
Appointment Book

date
_____

time	task	status

to do list:

_____ □
_____ □
_____ □
_____ □
_____ □
_____ □
_____ □
_____ □
_____ □

notes:

Executive Daily Planner and Appointment Book

date
_____

time	task	status

to do list:

_____ ☐
_____ ☐
_____ ☐
_____ ☐
_____ ☐
_____ ☐
_____ ☐
_____ ☐
_____ ☐

notes:

Executive Daily Planner and
Appointment Book

date _____

time	task	status

to do list:

_____ ☐
_____ ☐
_____ ☐
_____ ☐
_____ ☐
_____ ☐
_____ ☐
_____ ☐
_____ ☐

notes:

Executive Daily Planner and
Appointment Book

date

time	task	status

to do list:

_____ ☐
_____ ☐
_____ ☐
_____ ☐
_____ ☐
_____ ☐
_____ ☐
_____ ☐
_____ ☐

notes:

Executive Daily Planner and Appointment Book

date
_____

time	task	status

to do list:

_____ ☐
_____ ☐
_____ ☐
_____ ☐
_____ ☐
_____ ☐
_____ ☐
_____ ☐
_____ ☐

notes:

Executive Daily Planner and
Appointment Book

date

time	task	status

to do list:

☐
☐
☐
☐
☐
☐
☐
☐
☐

notes:

Executive Daily Planner and
Appointment Book

date
_____

time	task	status

to do list:

_____ ☐
_____ ☐
_____ ☐
_____ ☐
_____ ☐
_____ ☐
_____ ☐
_____ ☐
_____ ☐

notes:

Executive Daily Planner and
Appointment Book

date

time	task	status

to do list:

☐
☐
☐
☐
☐
☐
☐
☐
☐

notes:

Executive Daily Planner and
Appointment Book

date

time	task	status

to do list:

- _____ ☐
- _____ ☐
- _____ ☐
- _____ ☐
- _____ ☐
- _____ ☐
- _____ ☐
- _____ ☐
- _____ ☐

notes:

Executive Daily Planner and Appointment Book

date ____

time	task	status

to do list:

_____ ☐
_____ ☐
_____ ☐
_____ ☐
_____ ☐
_____ ☐
_____ ☐
_____ ☐
_____ ☐

notes:

Executive Daily Planner and Appointment Book

date
_____

time	task	status

to do list:

_____ ☐
_____ ☐
_____ ☐
_____ ☐
_____ ☐
_____ ☐
_____ ☐
_____ ☐
_____ ☐

notes:

Executive Daily Planner and
Appointment Book

time	task	status

to do list:

_____ ☐
_____ ☐
_____ ☐
_____ ☐
_____ ☐
_____ ☐
_____ ☐
_____ ☐
_____ ☐

notes:

Executive Daily Planner and Appointment Book

date
_____

time	task	status

to do list:

_____ ☐
_____ ☐
_____ ☐
_____ ☐
_____ ☐
_____ ☐
_____ ☐
_____ ☐
_____ ☐

notes:

Executive Daily Planner and
Appointment Book

date _____

time	task	status

to do list:

☐
☐
☐
☐
☐
☐
☐
☐
☐

notes:

Executive Daily Planner and
Appointment Book

date

time	task	status

to do list:

_____ ☐
_____ ☐
_____ ☐
_____ ☐
_____ ☐
_____ ☐
_____ ☐
_____ ☐
_____ ☐

notes:

Executive Daily Planner and
Appointment Book

date
_____

time	task	status

to do list:

_____ ☐
_____ ☐
_____ ☐
_____ ☐
_____ ☐
_____ ☐
_____ ☐
_____ ☐
_____ ☐

notes:

Executive Daily Planner and
Appointment Book

date
____

time	task	status

to do list:

_____ ☐
_____ ☐
_____ ☐
_____ ☐
_____ ☐
_____ ☐
_____ ☐
_____ ☐
_____ ☐

notes:

Executive Daily Planner and
Appointment Book

date _____

time	task	status

to do list:

_____ ☐
_____ ☐
_____ ☐
_____ ☐
_____ ☐
_____ ☐
_____ ☐
_____ ☐
_____ ☐

notes:

Executive Daily Planner and
Appointment Book

date
_____

time	task	status

to do list:

_____ ☐
_____ ☐
_____ ☐
_____ ☐
_____ ☐
_____ ☐
_____ ☐
_____ ☐
_____ ☐

notes:

Executive Daily Planner and
Appointment Book

date

time	task	status

to do list:

☐
☐
☐
☐
☐
☐
☐
☐
☐

notes:

Executive Daily Planner and
Appointment Book

date _____

time	task	status

to do list:

_____ ☐
_____ ☐
_____ ☐
_____ ☐
_____ ☐
_____ ☐
_____ ☐
_____ ☐

notes:

Executive Daily Planner and
Appointment Book

date ____

time	task	status

to do list:

_____ ☐
_____ ☐
_____ ☐
_____ ☐
_____ ☐
_____ ☐
_____ ☐
_____ ☐
_____ ☐

notes:

Executive Daily Planner and
Appointment Book

time	task	status

to do list:

notes:

Executive Daily Planner and
Appointment Book

time	task	status

to do list:

☐
☐
☐
☐
☐
☐
☐
☐
☐

notes:

Executive Daily Planner and
Appointment Book

date
_____

time	task	status

to do list:

_____ ☐
_____ ☐
_____ ☐
_____ ☐
_____ ☐
_____ ☐
_____ ☐
_____ ☐
_____ ☐

notes:

Executive Daily Planner and
Appointment Book

time	task	status

to do list:

notes:

Executive Daily Planner and
Appointment Book

date
___

time	task	status

to do list:

_____ □
_____ □
_____ □
_____ □
_____ □
_____ □
_____ □
_____ □
_____ □

notes:

Executive Daily Planner and
Appointment Book

date

time	task	status

to do list:

- [ ] _____
- [ ] _____
- [ ] _____
- [ ] _____
- [ ] _____
- [ ] _____
- [ ] _____
- [ ] _____
- [ ] _____

notes:

Executive Daily Planner and Appointment Book

date

time	task	status

to do list:

_____ ☐
_____ ☐
_____ ☐
_____ ☐
_____ ☐
_____ ☐
_____ ☐
_____ ☐
_____ ☐

notes:

Executive Daily Planner and
Appointment Book

date
_____

time	task	status

to do list:

_____ ☐
_____ ☐
_____ ☐
_____ ☐
_____ ☐
_____ ☐
_____ ☐
_____ ☐
_____ ☐

notes:

Executive Daily Planner and
Appointment Book

date

time	task	status

to do list:

_____ ☐
_____ ☐
_____ ☐
_____ ☐
_____ ☐
_____ ☐
_____ ☐
_____ ☐
_____ ☐

notes:

Executive Daily Planner and
Appointment Book

date
_____

time	task	status

to do list:

_____ ☐
_____ ☐
_____ ☐
_____ ☐
_____ ☐
_____ ☐
_____ ☐
_____ ☐
_____ ☐

notes:

Executive Daily Planner and
Appointment Book

date
_____

time	task	status

to do list:

_____ ☐
_____ ☐
_____ ☐
_____ ☐
_____ ☐
_____ ☐
_____ ☐
_____ ☐

notes:

Executive Daily Planner and
Appointment Book

date _____

time	task	status

to do list:

_____ ☐
_____ ☐
_____ ☐
_____ ☐
_____ ☐
_____ ☐
_____ ☐
_____ ☐
_____ ☐

notes:

Executive Daily Planner and
Appointment Book

date _____

time	task	status

to do list:

_____ ☐
_____ ☐
_____ ☐
_____ ☐
_____ ☐
_____ ☐
_____ ☐
_____ ☐
                    ☐

notes:

Executive Daily Planner and
Appointment Book

date
_____

time	task	status

to do list:

_____ ☐
_____ ☐
_____ ☐
_____ ☐
_____ ☐
_____ ☐
_____ ☐
_____ ☐
_____ ☐

notes:

Executive Daily Planner and
Appointment Book

date

time	task	status

to do list:

_____ ☐
_____ ☐
_____ ☐
_____ ☐
_____ ☐
_____ ☐
_____ ☐
_____ ☐
_____ ☐

notes:

Executive Daily Planner and Appointment Book

date
_____

time	task	status

to do list:

_____ ☐
_____ ☐
_____ ☐
_____ ☐
_____ ☐
_____ ☐
_____ ☐
_____ ☐
_____ ☐

notes:

Executive Daily Planner and
Appointment Book

date
____

time	task	status

to do list:

_____ ☐
_____ ☐
_____ ☐
_____ ☐
_____ ☐
_____ ☐
_____ ☐
_____ ☐
☐

notes:

Executive Daily Planner and
Appointment Book

date
_____

time	task	status

to do list:

_____ ☐
_____ ☐
_____ ☐
_____ ☐
_____ ☐
_____ ☐
_____ ☐
_____ ☐
_____ ☐

notes:

www.ingramcontent.com/pod-product-compliance
Lightning Source LLC
Chambersburg PA
CBHW080736250626
47170CB00010B/2851